More Tales of Irish Saints

More Tales
of Irish Saints

by ALICE CURTAYNE

Illustrated by Brigid Rynne

SHEED AND WARD - NEW YORK

Contents

49054

These Tales of Ireland's Golden Age are
  especially for:

The Gannon children of Boston

> Betsy
> Barbara
> Bob
> Mary Anne
> Jan

and for the Burke grandchildren of Chicago:

> Kathleen Carita
> Deirdre Ann
> Roger Joseph
> Maura Therese
> Gillian and
> John Burke Kiley

> John Joseph
> Mary Teresa
> Peter Francis
> Michael Vincent
> Paul Colum
> Mark James
> Thomas Joseph and
> Catherine Clare Gearen

> Deborah-Mary and
> Mara Ann Burke

with the writer's love.

More Tales of Irish Saints

Patrick's Rushes

When Saint Patrick was traveling around Ireland, converting the whole country to the Christian Faith, he did not travel alone. Far from it. He was at the head of a troop of people. First, he had a strong man, or bodyguard, who drove his chariot and helped him to ford the many bridgeless rivers and get through the forests which in those days covered Ireland. Then he had two or three priest companions to help with baptisms and confessions, when a great number of people were converted all at once. A school of boys also traveled with him; Patrick was training them to be priests, and as he could not stay in one place in order to do so, they had to come along. But what fun the traveling school must have been for the boys, who shared in the constant excitement of Patrick's missionary work!

Now this wasn't the lot, as there had to be a cook, too, to feed the company. There was also a carpenter

and a silversmith, because when Patrick converted
the people of a district, he did not leave until the
new Christians had a church. It was usually built
of wood, and the carpenter, who was skilled in this
work, took charge of it and saw that it was properly
done. Then the smith made the altar vessels and the
bell. Later on, the newly converted Christian women
were taught how to make the vestments and altar
cloths.

So you have to think of Patrick nearly always
surrounded by people, sometimes as many as fifty
of his own company, not to mention the converts
who crowded around him. Like all the saints of that
age, Patrick often felt the need to be alone. When
he got tired, he went away by himself to some quiet
place to pray and that always made him feel better
and able to start off again.

The story I am now going to tell you took place
when he was returning to his company after just such
a little rest by himself. It happened in that part
of Ireland now known as County Limerick, on the
road between Kilmallock and Kilfinane. It was
Christmas Eve. The short winter's day was already
closing in. Patrick was looking forward to spending
the morrow's great feast with his friends, and especially the boys. They were all guests in a chieftain's

fort and were being well looked after in the way of warm rooms and good food. Patrick was glad of this because the weather was severe.

He was making good speed when all at once it began to snow. This made the going very difficult. The road anyway was only a mere track, and now he could no longer see where he was going. The whirling flakes blotted out everything. He had to feel his way with his feet, which were sometimes on the track and sometimes squelching in the surrounding bogland. Now, although Patrick was tough and could stand cold and long journeys and going without his meals, on this occasion even he began to get anxious. Soon he realized that he was lost in a snowstorm and would never reach the chieftain's fort that night. He would have to get shelter somewhere.

He prayed for help as he plodded on, bent almost double as he tried to make headway against the driving snow. Then he saw a rough stone hut at the side of the road. It was only a dim outline and he had almost passed it before he noticed it. There was not a glimmer of light, or a sign of smoke from the chimney. He groped for the door and knocked. No answer. He knocked louder. Still no answer. Then he hammered at the door and at last a sleepy voice called out, "Who's there?"

"Please let me in out of the snowstorm," said Patrick.

There was the sound of shuffling inside and soon the door was opened by a man wrapped in a shepherd's cloak. He brought Patrick in, saying that he was welcome to share the hut for the night. The man was very poor, but kind. Patrick soon found out that there was no light to be had, no fire on the hearth, no food in the house. The man kept saying he was sorry.

Patrick was cold, hungry and tired. "Bring in some rushes," he said to the man, as he tried to stamp the snow from his feet and shake it from his cloak.

"Rushes won't burn," said the man.

"Bring them in, anyway," said Patrick.

The man groped his way out the door unwillingly and presently returned with an armload of rushes, covered with snow. Patrick piled them up in the empty hearth and at once they sprang into flame and began to burn merrily like good, dry logs. The best of it was that instead of burning away quickly, they lasted on, burning slowly and brightly. Now Patrick could see around him and the hut began to get warm.

"Rest yourself on this straw," said the man kindly. "It's a pity I have no food for you."

Just then there was a loud, sad *moo* outside the door. The shepherd quickly opened it again, and there stood a cow with a little calf shivering beside her.

"She must have strayed from the herd," said the shepherd. He let them in and made them comfortable in a corner, strewing the floor with some of the straw from his own bed. Then he noticed that the cow had not been milked, so he milked her and offered some of the milk to Patrick. After that, they all went to sleep.

Next morning the fire was still burning and the snow was over. The shepherd warmed some more milk for his visitor before he started out. He also asked him many questions. Patrick told him about the one true God. The man believed and was baptized.

The place where the saint was sheltered is known to this day in the Irish language as "the place where the green rushes burn." Although rushes everywhere else only smolder when you try to light them, they say that the rushes growing in this district *do* light up when put on the fire. Another strange thing is that a calf is always born on Christmas Eve on some farm in this neighborhood, no matter how the farmers there try to arrange things differently.

The Robber Who Became a Bishop

"Watch out for Maccul, the terrible Maccul of the One Eye! You'll want to be careful!"

Patrick was tired of that warning. He had told his friends that he was soon setting out for the north of Ireland, through County Down and then past the place which was to be known as Belfast nearly a thousand years later. Maccul indeed! Had not Patrick his own trusted bodyguard?

"Is it one bodyguard? Sure you'd need at least six strong men to protect you from Maccul and his robber gang," his friends told him. Patrick tossed his head and made a face, as much as to say, "I'll chance it!"

"All right," his friends said, "but remember you've been warned!"

This Maccul was a well-known highwayman who

roamed about the northeast of Ireland with his five or six followers, each of them just as bad as himself. They robbed everyone they met on the road, and anyone who put up a fight against them was nearly sure to be killed. The Maccul gang were all murderers. I need hardly tell you that outlaws of this kind were severely punished even in ancient Ireland, but it was very hard to capture Maccul. He was as slippery as an eel. He owned Island Mahee and four other islands in Strangford Lough. The best of an island is that you can see from it when a boat is coming, and you have plenty of time to get away if you want to. When the King's soldiers went searching for Maccul, he could go island hopping until they were tired of the chase. Indeed, that had already happened several times.

Patrick, however, was not put off by his friends. He set forth on his journey. He could not allow Maccul to prevent him from going on with his missionary work. His companions, however, were not as brave as he was. They were not happy on that road by the lough, when Island Mahee came into sight, and were probably silently praying that Maccul was far away in some other part of Ireland.

But Maccul was indeed very much at home; in fact, he was watching that road from his stronghold, while trying to make up his mind what robbery he could manage to do that day. It was with wicked delight that he saw the chariots of Patrick and his friends rounding the mainland road. The horses were going only at walking pace because they were tired. Island Mahee is close to the shore and Maccul knew he would have plenty of time to row across and cut off their advance. He told his man to get out the boat.

"It's not worth your while," said the man, who had also sighted the travelers. "That's only the Shaven One." This was one of the many names by which Patrick was known to the pagans in Ireland because, like all the monks of his time, the front of his head was shaved.

"The Shaven One! Who's he?" asked Maccul.

His man explained that Patrick was a priest from overseas, who went about Ireland telling people about the Christian Faith.

"He has no money," he ended up.

That should have closed the matter, because money was the only thing that mattered to the robbers. Still, Maccul was interested in an odd kind of way. He repeated the order to get out the boat.

"It's better to leave those men alone," his man advised him. "They are friendly with the High King and all the chieftains of Ireland. They have nothing of any use to us. I have been told, too, that that Patrick has strange powers. Someone even told me he could raise the dead to life!"

"Raise the dead to life! That's a good one! Let's go over and have some fun out of him. I have an idea. . . ." Maccul roared with laughter.

His man got out the boat and Maccul, with three of his band, went across to the mainland. On their way, they made up a plan. One of them named Garban would pretend to be dead. The others would cover him with a cloak, carry him on a plank to the foreign priest and beg him to raise the dead to life! At least they'd have a bit of sport, even if there was to be no robbery that day.

The Christians saw the boat putting out from the Island and their hearts sank. This was *it*—what all their friends had been warning them about—the terrible cutthroat, Maccul! Patrick alone did not seem disturbed. As they drew near the place where the boat had landed, what was their surprise to see the robbers, headed by Maccul, walking with their heads bowed in sorrow, carrying a bier. So many people had told them what Maccul was like that they knew him at once: he had only one eye and a terrible face.

"It's Maccul!" whispered Patrick's strong-man, getting ready his spear.

"Put away that weapon," Patrick told him.

The two groups, Patrick's and Maccul's, now faced each other on the road.

"Our friend is dead," whined Maccul, putting on an act. "Could you please bring him back to life again?"

"I am sorry he is dead," said Patrick, slowly and sternly, "even though you are only pretending that he is."

There was silence. The robbers stood back, very startled. What did he mean? The Christians passed on their way. Somehow the joke had fallen flat. The robbers laid the plank on the road and Maccul pulled the cloak off Garban.

"Get up out of that," he said crossly. He was annoyed because the fun he had expected had not come off. Garban did not move. His companions shook him hard, but it was of no use. He *was* dead! The three robbers bent over him; he was cold and stiff. They looked at one another. What kind of a man was that foreign priest who had such power....?

Maccul suddenly wheeled and tore along the road after Patrick, shouting, "Wait a minute! Stop!"

The driver reined in the horse. Robber and saint looked at each other. Then, to the great surprise of his companions, Maccul fell on his knees and asked Patrick to forgive him. He said he wanted to change his whole life and be a Christian. There was no pretending now. Anyone could see that he meant it.

"You have killed and robbed so many people," said Patrick sadly, "and you have led such a wicked life, you will have to do a great deal of penance."

Maccul said that if he could only be a Christian, he would do anything Patrick told him. He begged the saint to bring Garban back to life.

"It was my fault," he explained. "He was always afraid of me. I told him to play the trick."

Patrick stepped down from the chariot and walked back with Maccul to where Garban lay. He looked down at the robber for a moment and then raised his hand in blessing. Garban stirred. Then he sat up and stared around him.

I cannot tell you what happened to him and the other robbers afterward, but Maccul went off with Patrick, who baptized him. Later on, Maccul gave Patrick Island Mahee and his four other islands. Patrick founded a monastery on Island Mahee and left one of his priests to take charge of it.

In ancient Ireland, a great sinner like Maccul was sometimes punished by being cast away from Ireland in an open boat, without rudder or oars, and with his feet chained. The people would be rid of him and his wicked deeds forever, and there was a chance that he might live, if God so willed it. Maccul said that that form of punishment should be his penance. He had killed so many and stolen from so many more, he knew he would be always meeting people who hated his bad deeds of the past and who would find it hard to believe that he was now a good man.

Patrick agreed that it was better for Maccul to leave Ireland. He stood on the shore looking on, when Maccul's feet were chained together and the former robber was placed sitting in an open boat that had neither rudder nor oars. This was cast adrift on an ebbing tide when a strong wind blew from the west. Maccul was not afraid. He said that he deserved to be drowned in punishment for his sins, but that he would pray for God's mercy as long as he was alive. Patrick watched the boat until it was carried so far out to sea that it was lost to view. Then he went away alone and prayed earnestly for Maccul's safety.

The boat was not lost. It drifted to the Isle of Man, in the Irish Sea, and at length was cast up on a broad beach. There were Christian missionaries on the Isle who had already converted most of its people. Maccul was kindly received by the Christian inhabitants. They took the chains off his feet and gave him food and a home. Later on, he told the missionaries the whole story of his life. They taught him how to lead a good Christian life. He did penance for his sins for many years and then he became a monk.

When the missionaries died, Maccul took their place as leader of the Isle of Man Christians. He was their first bishop. After his death, he was revered as a saint. If you ever visit that island, you will find there many memorials of him, including the ruins of a very ancient church. Also a well, a headland, a little bay, a parish and a barony are all called after Saint Maccul, so that his name should never be forgotten.

Carthage and the Druid

Saint Patrick, when converting the Irish to Christianity, always made sure that there were no statues of pagan gods left in the place where he had preached and baptized. He was very strict about this because he wanted the Irish to make a completely new start, and to have nothing to do with paganism ever again. Nevertheless, long after Patrick's death, there were many Druids, or priests, of the old pagan religion left in the country. They hated the Christians and did everything they could to harm them.

One early spring day, Carthage was praying alone in his garden when he saw one of those Druids looking sourly at him through the gate. This Druid was also a magician, but Carthage was not in the least afraid. He asked him gently if he wanted to know anything about Our Lord, Who died for us.

"I won't believe unless I see miracles," snapped the Druid.

"What do you want me to do?" asked Carthage.

"Bring out leaves on that apple tree over there," said the Druid.

It was not the season yet for leaves, indeed the buds were not even open but still tight and hard. Carthage looked at the bare tree. Then he made the Sign of the Cross over it, and immediately it was covered with green leaves. A tree in full leaf in a garden where all the other trees had only bare branches! But the Druid only made a face.

"It would be more beautiful with blossoms on it," he said with a sniff.

Again Carthage made the Sign of the Cross over the tree, and at once it was covered with masses of delicate white, pink-tipped blossoms. The Druid did not seem in the least impressed.

"It would be better," he sneered, "if there were apples on it."

Once more Carthage blessed the tree in the name of Christ, and the white and pink blossoms changed into apples. The Druid's face was still grim; he seemed determined not to be pleased.

"It would be better if the apples were ripe," he said.

Before Carthage could lift his hand again in blessing, the apples began to plop down on the grass under the tree. They were golden ripe and juicy. Carthage picked one up and silently offered it to the Druid. He took it, but without so much as saying 'Thanks.' When he stuck his teeth in it, he made an awful face and gave an angry shout. "This apple is sour!"

Carthage blessed the apples and immediately they tasted sweet as honey.

So the Druid went off munching his apple, but still grumbling, still refusing to believe. "I could," he said over his shoulder to Carthage, "work far better magic than that!"

But the Druid had not gone far before he was suddenly stricken with blindness. It was a punishment for refusing to believe in the evidence of his eyes. With all his boasts about magic, he could not cure himself; neither could any of his Druid friends.

For a whole long year the unbelieving Druid was stone blind and had to be led around from place to place. At length he made up his mind to go back to Carthage and humbly ask him to cure his sight. The saint gently touched the Druid's eyes while saying a prayer and once more he could see. It was wonderful to see the world again: the kindly face of Carthage, the garden, the apple trees (now bare of leaves), the bright sky and the white clouds over all. The Druid was very thankful to Carthage and he at last really believed in Our Lord, Who had given such power to His priests.

Ciaran's Blackberries

Ciaran lived about the same time as Saint Patrick, in the fifth century. Like nearly all the saints of Ireland's Golden Age, he began his priestly life by living apart from other people. He prayed a great deal, striving to get to know God, so that he would be good at bringing sinners to Him.

He had built for himself a small hut in a wood near the river Nanny at Duleek. Here he lived on whatever food he could find for himself: the brown trout that he caught in the river, herbs, nuts and wild raspberries. One day he was walking through the wood when he saw clusters of ripe blackberries. This was something new and he thanked God for the gift. He ate as much of them as he wanted and then took careful note of where they grew. He put a bundle of rushes over the bush so that he would have no diffi-

culty in finding it again and using up all the blackberries before the winter came.

But every time he went back to this bush, he found
ripe blackberries there, waiting for his hand to pluck
them. At first he thought it was because the bush was
protected by the rushes. But when the snow came
and all the other bushes were bare and desolate,
Ciaran knew that his private store of blackberries
was a miracle, a token that he had found favor with
the Lord.

A chieftain named Concraid was the lord of all that
territory. He was a good Christian who loved having
the monk living on his land. He was proud of his
friendship with Ciaran. Now it happened that the
King and Queen of Munster came on a visit to Concraid. The Queen was called by the people of Ireland "Ethna the Horrible," not on account of her
face, which was nothing out of the ordinary, but
because of her unpleasant character. She was cruel;
she told lies; she was a mischief-maker; she was even
said to have caused wars.

All went well with the visit to Concraid until the
morning when the King and Queen were due to leave
again. Then Ethna did not get up. She said she could
not move her body and that she was sick. The King
had to go away without her because he had many

things waiting to be done at home. Concraid's servants did all they could for the Queen, but she did not seem to improve. The truth, however, was that she was perfectly well, and was only pretending to be sick so that she could stay on longer, because she was tired of her own place in Munster.

Concraid was terribly worried. He knew her bad name as a mischief-maker and he was most anxious to get her out of his house as quickly as possible. He went to her room and said to her very politely that he was very sorry she was sick, and could he do anything to make her better?

"If you could get me a plate of blackberries," said Ethna, "they would be medicine and healing herbs to me, I long for them so much."

Worse and worse, thought poor Concraid to himself. It was the month of April and the leaves on the blackberry bushes were only in bud. There would be no fruit on them until August, at the earliest. Concraid's heart sank at the thought of having Ethna the Horrible as his guest for four months, upsetting his household and getting him into all kinds of trouble.

He rode off to the wood to seek advice from his friend, Ciaran. The saint was grilling a trout over the open fire for his supper. Concraid thought nothing was tastier than brown trout grilled over a wood fire. Ciaran divided his supper with him and the two men, chieftain and saint, had a happy time together. Then Concraid told Ciaran the awful trouble he was in, with Ethna the Horrible likely to be his guest for months and months on end.

"I'll be lucky," he said, "if she does not cause a war here before I can get her back to her husband. She says she won't get better until blackberries are found for her." He made a face as he said this, because he thought blackberries an impossible thing to ask for.

"Blackberries!" Ciaran's smile flashed out. "That's easy!" The friends were sitting on the river bank where rushes were growing. Ciaran pulled up a bunch of them and quickly wove them into a basket. Then he led his friend to his special blackberry bush, from which he filled the basket. He blessed the fruit before he gave it to Concraid.

The surprised chieftain carried home the precious fruit as quickly as he could and sent it to Ethna's room with his compliments. It was her turn to be surprised, but she pretended to be pleased, and she had to eat the blackberries because the servants were standing around the bed waiting for her to do so.

At the first mouthful she said, "M-m-m, delicious!" Those strange blackberries had the scent of wine and the taste of honey, but best of all was Ciaran's blessing on them. It was that which changed the heart of Ethna the Horrible, and turned her from a bad woman into a good one. She rose up at once and said she wanted to go back to her own kingdom.

Concraid came then to bid her farewell. She asked him where he had found the wonderful fruit and he told her. So, before returning to Munster, Ethna called on Ciaran to give thanks to God and to him. She went to confession and after that she never made any more mischief, but lived a holy life and had a happy death.

Berach and the Beer

This story happened at a time when all Ireland was ruled by a High King who lived in Tara, the royal palace in the middle of County Meath. Every year, just after Easter, the King gave a wonderful feast to his people, who came from all parts of the island to enjoy themselves. They camped around the Hill of Tara and for three days they had games and sports and a feast. There was perfect peace, too, because the law said that everyone had to forget their quarrels for those three days. It was a good idea because sometimes, when quarrels are put aside for three days, they are forgotten forever.

During the rest of the year, the King went on visits to the great chieftains, whenever his business as ruler made it necessary. When this happened, the chieftain who was to receive him would be told a long time ahead, because the King traveled with a large number of soldiers and servants, perhaps as many as a hundred, so that great preparations had to be made. Then the chieftain's household would set to work like mad, preparing food for a great banquet and polishing up the whole place. The High King set them such a good example at Tara, everyone felt bound to copy him.

Saint Berach was at this time abbot of several monasteries. One day he had to visit one of the houses of monks who were under his rule. The place that he had to get to was thirty miles away. Berach had to do the journey on foot. It was a long walk. Indeed, it was a walk that probably took the whole day, if Berach's pace was the same as yours and mine —three miles to the hour.

He set off at dawn, a lovely summer dawn which made him feel happy and lighthearted. He said all his prayers and he praised God for the beauty of the world. But later on, as the sun rose higher and higher in the sky, it became very warm and walking was not so easy. Several times Berach sat down by the roadside to rest, wiped his forehead and his neck, which were wet with sweat, and shook the dust out of his sandals. But as he wanted to end his journey by nightfall, he could not afford long rests.

Presently he became very thirsty. It is, as you probably know, a very uncomfortable feeling. Berach's lips became so dry that he could not close them, and his tongue felt as if it was too big for his mouth. The worst of it was that there was no water anywhere to be seen on that route: no rivers, no streams, no little flagstone-covered wells by the wayside. He kept leaving the road and searching the fields for a trickle of water. But he had no success. All the land was just baked up in the summer heat.

Presently he came to the gate of a chieftain's fort and he was delighted. "Here, anyhow," he said to himself, "I'll get a drink and then I can make some speed again." The gates were wide open, which was unusual. Berach knew that this meant someone important was expected. No one challenged him, so he went right up to the house.

The place was as busy as a beehive on a summer's day. Servants were running about in all directions, each of them intent on doing some urgent job. No one greeted him and when he tried to stop one of the men to ask for a drink, the man did not even hear him. Then the monk went straight into the banquet hall, where another troop of servants were busy making ready a great long table running down the center of the room. From the kitchens at the back of the hall came a delicious smell of cooking: boiled salmon, roast beef, baked apples. But what Berach found most interesting were the great vats of beer, fifty of them, ranged down along the walls. This was certainly going to be a tremendous feast!

In those days the Irish made their own beer in their homes from barley which they grew themselves. The chieftain's beer looked wonderful to Berach, now almost fainting from thirst; it was a deep golden color, sparkling, cool, with a creamy foam on top. A long, long drink of it would be just the thing to revive him and help him to finish the journey in the heat and dust.

"Could you give me a drink?" he asked one of the servants, who was carrying benches to put alongside the table. The man seemed neither to see him, nor to hear him.

"Could you *please* give me a drink?" he asked the next one, who was helping to strew fresh rushes on the floor.

The man gave him a kind of desperate look. "Get out of here," he said, "can't you see we're in a hurry?"

"What does he want?" asked his companion over his shoulder.

"A drink, please," said the first servant, imitating Berach's pleading tones.

"Don't you know that the High King is coming?" said a third man. "He'll be here any minute now. Clear out before you're kicked out."

A steward was fussing up and down the hall, seeing that everything was in order. "What's the trouble here?" he said to Berach.

"Could I have a drink?" said the monk again.

"NO-O-O!" roared the steward.

The servants laughed. Berach turned away. He said in a low, sad tone, "One drink to the Lord's servant would not have spoiled the King's feast."

So he walked out of the inhospitable place again. Just as he reached the gates, the King and his retinue arrived. Berach had to flatten himself against the wall to get out of the horses' way. When they had passed, Berach continued his walk, sucking grasses and chewing crab apple twigs as he went along to try and relieve his painful thirst.

But the King riding in his chariot had become nearly as thirsty as the man on foot. The horses' hoofs had kicked up an awful lot of dust which he could not avoid swallowing, and the heat had been intense. When he arrived at the door, the chieftain ran out to meet him, bowing low and bidding him welcome. The King cut short the compliments by saying just what poor Berach had said, "Could I have a drink, please? The dust on the road and the heat have made me dry."

So the chieftain immediately sent a servant to bring a drink of beer from the banquet hall. To his surprise the servant found the first vat empty, and the second one and the third! Then he ran right around the hall, looking into all the vats. But every single one of them was drained empty and dry.

The servant began shouting to the others and you never heard such a commotion and hubbub. All the servants were running from vat to vat, shouting at the steward, who was running around in circles as if he was out of his mind. Could all the vats have been leaking? He tried to find someone to blame. He did the silliest things, like going down on all fours to look at the floor under the vats, and even behind them! He could not believe that there was only water in the fort to offer the King! This was the bad news the servant brought back to the chieftain who, naturally enough, was furious and who tried hard not to prance about with rage like the steward had done. But there was no help for it; the King just had to be told, and ordinary, dull water was poured into his goblet instead of the sparkling beer with a creamy top.

Now the King was a Christian, but the chieftain

was not. The King was used to the ways of monks and especially saints. He began to suspect something. He asked his host, had anyone been into the hall to interfere with the vats. The chieftain summoned the steward and the waiters to report on this. At first they said it was quite impossible, that no one could have touched the vats except themselves. Then the steward suddenly remembered the meek figure of the monk, whom he had roared at and put out on the road.

"Ah, well, yes," he stammered, "a man did come in a little while ago. He looked like a student. He was carrying a little bell and a staff. He asked for a drink and went away sadly when we refused him."

"That's it," said the King at once. "It is he who has ruined the feast. Go after him and bring him back. We'll have to get his blessing and forgiveness."

One of the servants sprang on a horse and, leading another mount, he galloped off. Finding out by inquiry the direction taken by Berach, he soon overtook him and begged him to go back with him, as the High King wanted him. Berach agreed and mounted the other horse.

Meanwhile, the King sipped the water and patiently waited. When he heard the sound of the horses' hoofs, he went out and knelt down before Ber-

ach, whom he knew, asking his forgiveness for what
had been done to him in that place today. The monk
smiled and went back to the hall, where he made the
Sign of the Cross over the empty vats, which immediately filled up with beer. You can imagine how the
servants—who had been so rude to him the first time
—crowded around him now, pressing him to have a

drink. Berach smilingly accepted. Then he slipped
out of the fort and went on his way on foot as before.

After that, the feast got under way in the hall and
everyone was happy. But the chieftain was bothered.
He was astonished at what he had seen and he plied
the King with questions about the Christian God
Who gave such power to His servants. Some time
later, the chieftain was converted with all his family.

Then he sent for Berach, asking him to visit his fort again. This time it was not only a drink he gave him, but enough land for another monastery and church, promising that he and his heirs would protect and support it forever and ever.

Brendan and the Whale

There was a legend in Ireland, going back to the very dawn of time, that somewhere beyond the great western ocean was a wonderful land, abounding in riches, where the sun shone all the year round and where fruit and flowers were as plentiful as in the Garden of Eden. The Irish people called this imaginary country *Hy-Brasil,* which means Land of the Blessed.

Brendan was born in Kerry, a part of southwest Ireland which sends out long fingers of headlands, as if it was trying to feel for another country across the wide sea. When he was a boy, he often gazed out to the west over the Atlantic Ocean, straining his eyes to see a sign of land beyond the horizon. He wondered and wondered about the beautiful place the old people talked about, and he longed with all his young heart to be able to see it.

When Brendan grew up to be a man, he became a
monk. But his new way of life hardly made any differ-
ence; he still longed to be an explorer, he still longed
to discover if there was any truth in that legend about
the Land of the Blessed beyond the rim of the ocean.

One day he turned to his friends in the monastery
and surprised them by saying, "I will go myself and
find Hy-Brasil."

No one said anything for a few minutes and then
they all spoke together, telling him that he was mad,
quite, quite mad to even think of such a wild scheme.
But they soon grew silent again, for each one was
turning over in his own mind the idea of this ad-
venture. Brendan was, of course, a very good sailor;
he was skilled in making boats and was very clever
about the art of directing a course by the stars. He
was also a man without fear. But then again, such a
journey would take days and nights, weeks and weeks,
even months and months; it would be endless. Well,
supposing he had enough food with him in the boat,
the time would not matter. But supposing there were
great storms, hurricanes—he wouldn't have a chance
to live through these in an open boat. Suppose his
boat struck an iceberg; suppose he got lost. . . . There
was no end to the dreadful "supposing."

"Don't be foolish, Brendan," they said. "You

would never get even half way to Hy-Brasil." But
he only smiled. Soon after that he set about making
preparations. He was determined to make an attempt
to find the legendary land, no matter how much he
was discouraged.

The first thing he did was to build what seemed to
the people of that time a tremendous boat, big enough,
indeed, to hold about twenty people and all the food
and fresh water required for a long voyage. The news
of Brendan's new boat and of his plan to sail across
the Atlantic soon got around to all the other Irish
monasteries. And everywhere the monks who had
been seafaring men before they entered the monasteries became excited. A monk leaving his quiet life
of prayer and going off to a foreign country! It was
great and stirring news and many holy men began to
feel envious. "And," said they, "he is perfectly right
to go. There may be people in Hy-Brasil who have
never heard of Christ. He can preach to them and
save their souls."

Brendan building a boat to sail to the edge of the
world where the evening sun disappeared! The excitement spread, and soon many monks began to ask
leave to go with Brendan. When they came to him,
he was gay and said, "Yes, to be sure—if you are
good at the oars." Presently he had as many com-

panions as his boat would hold. Then he had to say, "No, very sorry, but we have a full boat already." Perhaps he asked the disappointed ones to pray hard for his success in finding Hy-Brasil.

Soon all was ready. The boat was packed with food, casks of fresh water, ropes, carpenters' tools and all the things necessary for a long sea voyage. Brendan and his monks set out from Kerry across a great sea with nothing but a sort of fairy-tale land at the other side.

They had been at sea for a very long time and had grown weary of seeing nothing but wastes of water day after day. They longed for the sight of land and they longed to be able to stretch their legs. It was Holy Week and more than ever they longed for a piece of dry land where they could celebrate the Easter Mass. They prayed as they pulled the oars, of course, and many is the time they raised their eyes to search the horizon wistfully. At dawn on Easter Sunday, they were overjoyed to see what looked like a small, rather round, rather shiny, island nearby. They immediately put up more sails and rowed as hard as they could.

Yes, it was a little island, but completely bare, without grass or trees. And although they went all around it, they could discover no place that would serve as a landing stage; there was not even a sandy edging as there is on other islands. But they were delighted and all, except Brendan, who remained in the boat, scrambled on to the land. Soon the monks fixed up an altar and Mass was celebrated, the lovely Easter Mass with its joyful hymns and prayers.

After Mass, the monks decided that they would have a meal, the first meal on dry land for goodness knows how many days. They carried the big pot from the boat, and with some chips and scraps started a fire; they planned to have a grand breakfast of boiled fish.

But the island had other plans! As soon as the fire began to blaze, the whole island went into a kind of shiver and pot, fire and monks began to wobble. This island was alive! The terrified monks appealed to Brendan to save them; he held out his hands and pulled them into the boat. The moment the last man had his foot on the gunwale, the whole island dived to the bottom of the sea! I don't think I have to tell you it was no real island, but an enormous whale. The whale, which looked like an island, slept quietly while Mass was being said, but it very naturally objected to having a fire lighted on its back. And who would not?

Some time later and after many more adventures, Brendan and his companions found themselves sailing along in a frightening darkness which lasted day and night. They, of course, lost all sense of direction. All they could do was to go with the wind and pray Heaven for help. At last, when the darkness cleared, they saw a beautiful shore stretching as far as eye could see. It was journey's end and the other side of the vast Atlantic. They laughed and sang and cheered as they pulled their boat out of the sea on to the beach.

They set about examining this new country. It was rich and beautiful; the sun was warm and brilliant. In the days to come, the monks were to discover that this new-found land was vast and varied, full of every sort of delicious fruit, wild corn and edible roots; the rivers abounded in fish and the forests in wild animals.

Brendan and his monks traveled in this land for forty days and forty nights and, according to the story they brought home to Ireland, the sun shone every day. The forty days were all too short (they said) because there was so much to look at, and everything seemed so fresh and lovely after the weeks and weeks at sea.

Was it the famous Hy-Brasil? At any rate, it was a huge country. At length the travelers came to a mighty river which seemed to run through the middle of the land. They could not cross it because it was so wide. "We will never be able to discover the limits of this great country," said the monks. And so they decided to return to the place where they had drawn up their boat, and go back to Ireland.

In after ages it was often said that the land described by Brendan and his monks was the United States of America and that the mighty river was the Mississippi. Curiously enough, many Indian tribes told an ancient tale that had come down through the ages of peaceful white men, using iron tools, arriving in their midst after traveling a long way across the sea.

Why Brendan Hated Music

Brendan, the great sailor saint, gave up sea voyages when he got old. He then stayed quietly in one place, Clonfert, the monastic school he had founded in the center of Ireland, far from either sight or sound of the sea he had loved so much. Perhaps he went so far away from the sea toward the end of his life as an extra penance. At Clonfert, he taught in the school, worked beside the other monks and prayed a great deal. He was good company, however, and never ran short of exciting tales: sea-thrillers of sharks and whales, icebergs, monsoons, waterspouts, monsters and strange lands.

But he had one queer habit which puzzled the other monks: he did not like music. When anyone began to sing, or to play on the harp, he would walk out of the room with his hands to his ears. Now the Irish have always been noted for their love of music and the monks did not like the Father Abbot to behave in this way. When visitors came and gave a concert to the monks, Brendan was never present, no matter how they pleaded with him.

The monks would say to him: "But Father Abbot, this harpist is the best in Ireland. He can charm the very birds off the trees. Just listen to him for a moment. . . ." or, "This man sings for the High King. He's really first-rate. Just hear him for yourself. . . ."

Brendan would only shake his head and look miserable. Worse than that, he made two little balls of wax and fastened them together with string. He kept these in his Mass-book like a bookmarker. When the monks chanted the psalms in church, he would put the balls of wax in his ears so that he could not hear them. You will agree that this was not very polite.

One Easter Sunday morning, the monks had been celebrating the Resurrection of Our Lord with special devotion. First, they had said the psalms together at dawn; then they had heard Mass and received Holy Communion; then they had listened to a very long sermon and, finally, they had said the Office together. At last it was midday and they went to the refectory for the Easter feast. Alleluia! Now was the time to celebrate the joys of Easter.

After the feast, a young novice who had only lately come to Clonfert offered to play the harp. He was an excellent musician and soon they were all clapping and cheering him. He was very obliging. He played the airs of songs they could sing together; he played merry music that made them laugh, and sad music that made them thoughtful. They had a happy time.

Brendan, of course, was not present. He had remained on in the church, praying. The young novice missed him and asked why he did not come. The others explained to him Brendan's odd habit where music was concerned. The young musician was downcast.

"Perhaps I could change him," he said. "I do not want to boast, but I could have been the King's minstrel if I had not made up my mind to be a priest."

The older monks shook their heads, but the boy continued to urge that the Father Abbot be coaxed to join them at their Easter feast. He said, "I will take my harp into the church and play a few airs for him. I am sure he will listen to me."

They told him it would be of no use, but the boy was a good sort who never liked to give up without trying. First tuning his harp carefully, he carried it to the church. The door was bolted on the inside.

"Open," he called out boldly.

"Who is there?" asked Brendan.

"A young novice to play the harp for you."

"Play it outside!" said Brendan.

"If you don't mind," insisted the young man, "I would be grateful if you would allow me into the church to play it there for you."

"Very well," said Brendan, as he opened the door.

The boy sat down beside his harp, determined to put his very soul into the music. But Brendan slipped the little balls of wax into his ears.

"Oh," cried the boy sadly, "I can't play for you unless you take those things out of your ears!"

"Very well," said Brendan again. He removed the balls of wax.

The novice then played his three favorite tunes— lovely haunting tunes, sweet and low. But all the time Brendan listened with a look of pain on his face, as if he had a toothache, or maybe it would be better to call it what it was, earache. All the same, when the music was ended, he said politely, "A blessing on you now, and the music of heaven to you hereafter."

He replaced the balls of wax and the look on his face said plainly, "Go away, because I cannot bear any more of it."

The young novice was almost crying, he was so disappointed. "Why don't you like my music?" he said. "Is it because you think it is *bad* music?"

Brendan had a kind heart and he was sorry for the

well-meaning lad. "No," he said gently. "It's not that. But seven years ago this very Easter day, I was here in this church after Mass. All the others had gone to their dinner, just like today, and I remained here alone because, after my Communion, a great longing for my Lord had seized hold of me. I fell into a state of fear and trembling. Then I saw a bird on the window. It flew in and rested on the high altar. I could not look at it because of the sun-bright beams around it.

'Give me thy blessing, O monk,' said the bird.

'God bless you,' said I. 'Who are you?'

'Michael the Archangel,' he said. 'I have come to talk to you.'

'I thank God indeed,' I answered. 'And why did you come?'

'To bless you,' he said, 'and to play to you for thy Lord.'

'You are welcome,' I told him.

"Then he drew his beak across his outstretched wing and I heard the music of Heaven, and I listened till the same hour on the following day and then he bade me farewell."

There was a pause. The young harpist did not know what to say to the wonderful story. Then Brendan hit the bookcover against the side of the

harp, making a jangling noise. "Does that sound sweet to you?" he asked.

The boy shook his head.

"I tell you before God," said Brendan seriously, "that is how the music of this world sounds to me, ever since I heard the music made by Michael the Archangel." He turned away, saddened by the memory. Then he said, "But take my blessing and Heaven be yours in return for playing to me."

The boy reported to the monks the story Brendan had told him. Now they understood. Music would never be music for their Abbot until he heard it again in Heaven.

Columcille and the Flounders

I hope you have some idea what a flounder looks like; if not, it will be hard for you to enjoy the story of Saint Columcille and the flounders. Flounders are flatfish; so are sole, plaice and halibut. All these fish are very good to eat but very funny to look at. But perhaps you have caught one of these flatfish at some time yourself. They are easily captured; all you have to do is paddle at the edge of the sea, at a place where the bottom is fairly muddy. When you feel a wiggling under your feet, stoop down quickly and seize. You will have caught a queer-looking creature.

Now, when you have the flounder safe in your hand and begin to examine it, you will say, "This is his back, this is his front and, oh, what a crooked mouth he has!" You will be right about his mouth, but you will be wrong about his back and front. A flatfish's back is one of its sides, and what we call the front, or lower surface, is its other side!

I know you are thinking that I am saying something ridiculous, as if I said that this page's real sides were the edges. But it is not so ridiculous: you see, for the first month of its life, the flounder is like any other fish and has its sides at its sides. Then it swims down to the bottom of the sea and lies on one side. While lying in this way, three very strange changes take place. First, one side of the flounder changes color. Then, it changes its way of swimming, and wiggles along instead of swimming swiftly like any other fish. The last change is the oddest of all: the lower eye, the one against the bottom of the sea when the fish lay down, begins to move around the head, till at last it settles down by the side of the other eye!

I don't know exactly why the flounder's mouth is so crooked, but I suppose it has something to do with the traveling eye—indeed, the flounder's nose is very bent, too. However, there is a legend to explain the whole matter: how the flounders were impudent to Saint Columcille and how he punished them for being so.

Now, you must first know that Saint Columcille was a very handsome man. He was tall, strong and as straight as a spear; his face, it is said, beamed with holy joy and gladness. Saint Columcille, indeed, was a prince; his father was the great-grandson of King Niall of the Nine Hostages and his mother belonged to the royal house of Leinster. He *looked* every inch a prince.

One day the saint was walking beside the sea when he came on a shoal of flounders. There seemed to be hundreds and hundreds of them, all wiggling off in the same direction. Columcille watched them for a while, and then he said to one of them, "Are you all moving house, flounder?" He asked the question very politely and quietly and he did not deserve the pert answer he got.

"Yes, we are, crooked legs!"

"If I have crooked legs, may you have a crooked mouth!" said Columcille.

That is the reason the flounder has a crooked mouth.

Faelain's Three Wishes

The valley of Glendalough in County Wicklow is one of the most beautiful places in the whole world. A slender round tower, the ruins of a cathedral and of six other churches may be seen there on the shores of two lakes; a singing river splashes down from the wooded hills. Although this valley is nowadays crowded with sightseers from spring to autumn, its peace is unspoiled. It is still full of the presence of holy Saint Kevin, who first chose it for his home thirteen hundred years ago.

The kings of Ireland sometimes had an awkward way of showing their love for the saints. The King of Leinster at that time was very proud to have a famous saint like Kevin living in his kingdom, and nothing would do but to send his little grandson, aged six, to the monastic school to be trained. Since the

King's word was law, there was no choice. Whether he liked it or not, Kevin had to take the child. But the school was for boys of twelve and up and it seemed that the little prince, Faelain, was likely to be nothing but a trouble to the monks. However, Kevin gave the child into the care of one of the youngest monks in the school and hoped for the best.

Just at the same time, Saint Berach happened to be visiting Glendalough. He was strolling happily around the lake with his friend, Kevin, when they heard Faelain crying at the top of his voice. The gentle Kevin was troubled and both of them went back to find out what was wrong. Faelain wanted milk! He had been used to drinking lots of it when in his nurse's care in the royal palace. But there was very little milk in the monastery, if indeed there was any at all. The monks used to drink beer made from barley. On special feast days, they drank mead, a delicious drink made from fermented honey. They always had plenty of honey from the beehives they kept in the garden. But they had no cows and they did not care if they ever saw milk.

But Faelain wanted milk and nothing else. When he understood that there was no milk for him, he yelled. No milk! What a place to bring him! The young monk who had charge of him tried to coax him to drink mead, but the little boy pushed it away and cried louder still. It seemed likely that he would die of thirst, or possibly rage, if milk were not quickly found for him.

Kevin and Berach arrived at the spot. "Oh," said Kevin sadly, "he wants milk and there's none."

Berach thought for a moment. Then he lifted his hand and blessed the pine-clad mountain rising above the school. Almost at once a graceful little doe and her fawn trotted out from the shelter of the trees and came trustfully up to him. "The deer has milk for the child," said Berach.

The doe then stood over a hole in the rock—a round hole rather like a bowl—where she allowed herself to be milked. Then Faelain was called and a mug of milk taken out of the hollow for him. The boy's tears turned to laughter at sight of the doe and her fawn. He was gracious enough to say that the milk was really the very nicest that he had ever tasted.

The doe bounded off up the mountain again, followed by her fawn. The next morning she was back in the monastery enclosure, standing over the same hole in the rock, patiently waiting to be milked for Faelain. The same thing happened morning and evening for many weeks. Faelain was delighted. He would run out to stroke them and thank them. He was so pleased with his pets that he forgot the King's palace and he was not lonely any more.

But one day a sad thing happened. The doe came alone to the monastery, trembling with fright, and she had no milk to give. The monks guessed that a wolf must have killed and eaten her little fawn. Berach was told the sad news. Once again he looked up at the mountain, made the Sign of the Cross and said, "Let the animal who did a bad deed do a good one now."

Soon the wolf slunk out from the trees and settled himself on his paws before the doe, as if asking her pardon. Then a strange thing happened between those two animals who are usually enemies. The doe showed no sign of fright, but licked the wolf's head as though in forgiveness. A little later she allowed herself to be milked as usual. The same thing happened morning and evening for several weeks. The doe would arrive at the monastery, followed by the wolf, who would lie down in front of her until she was milked.

All that happened one thousand three hundred years ago, but if you visit Glendalough today, you will be shown the hole in the rock over which the doe used to stand to give milk for Faelain.

One winter's evening, Kevin heard the little boy

crying loudly again. The sound of a child crying was hateful to him. He sent to ask what was wrong. He was told that the boy had a pain and was asking for sorrel to cure it. Sorrel, of all things! It is a small plant rather like the shamrock, only it has bigger leaves. When eaten raw it has a bitter taste and is said to be good for curing windy pains and headaches. Whenever Faelain had a pain at home, his nurse had made him eat sorrel. He knew what to do to cure himself.

The monks told him there was no sorrel in Glendalough. What a place to bring him! He howled with rage. Again Berach and Kevin looked at each other. What are we to do? It's a simple thing he wants. Berach raised his hand in blessing, this time over a hump of rock near the monastery and there was the sorrel growing on it! Faelain had all he wanted of the bitter stuff. What is more, sorrel grows to this very day on that unlikely hump of rock to remind us of the miracle.

Another day, Berach and Kevin were talking under a beautiful willow tree in the garden. Faelain was playing near them, and presently he ran over and said he wanted some apples off the willow tree. They could have told him severely that he was a silly boy to think that apples could grow on willow trees, but they only smiled. Faelain began to cry. Indeed, he was good at crying. Kevin looked miserable, but Berach blessed the tree. Immediately apples were growing on it. He picked a few and gave them to Faelain, who of course stopped crying to eat them. The same willow tree continued to bear apples every autumn for hundreds of years afterward and people came from afar to see the wonder. They were curious apples, too, long in shape, whitish when ripe and never very sweet.

Such were Faelain's three wishes: for milk, for sorrel and for apples from a willow tree. I have never yet met a small boy who would not agree with him about the milk and the apples, but about the sorrel I am not so sure.

Brigid and the Minstrels

This is the story of how Saint Brigid once saved a man's life by means of music.

He was a shepherd slave who had been condemned to death by his master because a number of sheep were found missing from the flock. They *could* have been stolen during the night while the slave was asleep, but the master said they must have been eaten by wolves on the mountain because the slave was careless and did not mind them properly.

Slaves in Ireland were badly treated in those days. All the first Christians were very sorry for them, especially Saint Patrick, who understood their life because he himself had been a slave. The Christians tried very hard to bring in laws that would put an end to slavery and they succeeded, too. Slavery came to an end in Ireland hundreds of years before it ended in other countries.

The wife and children of the slave sentenced to death came to Brigid in her convent, begging her to help them in this terrible business. They were Christians, but the man's master was a pagan and a hard man, who was feared by everyone. Brigid listened sadly to the story and promised them to do her best. She called for her chariot and driver, and with two of her nuns set off for the chieftain's fort.

She was politely received by the servants, who told her their master was out. He might be absent for some hours, but would she care to wait? They led the three nuns into the banquet hall and went away. Presently the chieftain's aged father, who had been told of the visitors, came in to greet them. He was a pleasant old man and was soon chatting away to the nuns. Brigid explained why they had called. He sighed and said there was very little hope. He admitted that the slave had been the best worker in the household and that everyone thought the sentence too severe.

Then the old man went on to tell Brigid that the chieftain's young wife had died over a year ago, and that since then the chieftain had never smiled. He had become sad and gloomy. Although the period of mourning was long over, there was never a laugh heard in that household now. There was no music, no songs, no happiness. The chieftain still lived with his sorrow and would allow no one in the fort to forget it.

Brigid listened to all this with the kindness for which she was famous. Then her eyes fell on two harps hanging on the wall.

"Could we not have some music now, while we're waiting?" she asked.

The old man sighed again. "I used to sing in my younger days," he said, "but for over a year now no minstrel has been allowed in this place, and at present there is no one here with the skill to play."

Two slave boys then came into the hall to prepare the table for the evening meal. They smiled agreement with the old man's words.

"Take down the harps and play for us," Brigid told them. They grinned foolishly and said they had never played and did not know how.

"If someone could play, I would sing for you," said the old man. "I think I still have a little voice left."

"Do as she tells you," said one of Brigid's nun companions to the boys. "She might give you the skill."

Rather unwillingly and still looking foolish, the slave boys lifted the harps off the wall. They sat down and nervously touched the strings. To their wonder and excitement they found that they could play! They had never had such fun. The nuns would hum an air for them and they found that they could play it even before they heard it to the end. Then the old man sang for the nuns. The other servants came in to listen. The nuns sang for the chieftain's household; some of the servants sang in return. It was a wonderful concert. When everyone was tired of singing, the boys played on and on, as though they could not stop playing. The hours flew by. Time always passes quickly when people are happy.

In the middle of all this, the chieftain returned. As he sprang off his horse, he heard the unusual sound of music from the banquet hall. He heard the laughter of his aged father. Suddenly he realized that he had not heard either of those sounds for a very long time. He stood listening outside the window as if he was rooted to the spot. He, too, had been a great lover of music before sorrow had made him sour. As he listened, a stone seemed to melt in his breast. He went into the banquet hall and, instead of stopping the concert, he joined in.

Later on, he thanked Brigid very pleasantly for having brought such happiness to his household. He was delighted to find that the boys could play. Encouraged by this, Brigid pleaded for the life of the slave condemned to die. In a little while, the chieftain agreed to pardon him and even to give him his liberty.

Then Brigid told him about Christ Our Lord, Who died for us. He listened intently and promised to think about it. Some time later, he and his father became Christians.

The two slave boys were converted, too, and they never again lost the miraculous skill given to them by Brigid. They, too, were given their freedom. They became great musicians and so were their children, and their children's children, for hundreds of years.

Moling and the Wild Dogs

There is a dreaming place, called Saint Mullins, on the River Barrow in County Carlow. The river slopes are wooded and the river itself is very dark and slow moving. Always the place is peaceful and almost silent; herons fly with slow-beating wings from one side of the river to the other; moorhens call sudden *prruks* from the reeds, and the black, unruffled river reflects every leaf and twig of the overhanging trees. It was here that Saint Moling ruled as abbot of a monastery in the seventh century. He was very fond of animals and he had a great way with them, even wild and savage ones.

One day a pack of roving dogs, thirty in number, arrived at the monastery out of nowhere. Now, in many parts of the country there is a great fear of roving dogs, because of the harm they do to sheep. If these wild and bloodthirsty dogs get into a flock of sheep, there is no knowing what damage they will do, or how many lambs they will kill. The farmers around here often put pieces of poisoned meat in the fields for the dogs to eat; sometimes the farmers shoot the dogs. Roving dogs will attack people, too— no wonder there is fear of them. Saint Moling's monks were very much afraid of the dogs that rushed into the monastery, just as frightened as you or I would be. The dogs looked so fierce. They were so thin that all their ribs stood out; their tongues were hanging out of their mouths and they were panting hard, as if they had run a very long way.

"Savage dogs!" cried the monks. "Come quickly with some weapons!" But it was a useless shout because they had no weapons at all in the monastery. Those were the days when there was great peace in Ireland and monks and monasteries were loved by everyone.

If the monks were excited and afraid, Moling was as pleased as if a king had come to visit him. He immediately told the monks that the dogs were to be fed and made welcome. There were surprised looks on every face.

"Yes, I mean it. And give every dog a whole loaf of bread." Then he added with a big broad smile, "Be sure to put plenty of butter on the bread, too!"

Just think of that—butter! The monks obeyed,
although their looks plainly said that they thought
the abbot was far too generous, giving good bread
and valuable butter to a pack of stray dogs.

By the time the loaves and butter were brought
from the storehouse, some of the dogs, who had been
sniffing around the strange place, had strayed away
altogether. The monk who was carrying the food saw
that some dogs were missing and he looked at Moling

as much as to say, What do I do now? We could make a big saving because half the dogs have scattered. But Moling was not a man for doing generous things by halves.

"Leave it *all* there on the ground," he said to the monk. "They will come back for it."

The monk did what he was told. Meanwhile, the other monks gathered around to see what would happen next. What they saw was strange and unexpected. Instead of gobbling up all the food laid on the ground, the hungry dogs took only their share. Each dog ate just one buttered loaf and no more. And no snaps, snarls or growls. When they had finished their own share, they sat looking at the spare loaves with mournful eyes—looking, but not touching.

By and by the other dogs came back from their wandering and ate the share left for them. Moling was delighted with all this and threw back his head, laughing and laughing. I am afraid the rest of the monks only smiled slightly; they kept thinking that it was too much of a good thing to give wild dogs bread—with valuable butter on it!

Moling called the dogs to come around him, and he praised them for their good behavior and their nice table manners. They frisked about in great delight, all the long tails wagging together and dog-smiles on every dog face. It was a funny sight and the monks, every one of them, even the saving ones, all began to laugh. Then Moling blessed the dogs and sent them away.

Moling's Pet Fox

Like so many of the great Christian men of his time, Saint Moling's one desire was to get away from people and all the rush of business, so that he could live alone and spend all his time praising God. So he went off into a forest searching for a place where he could build a little house for himself away from crowds. As he went along, praying that God would direct him to a suitable place, he came upon an immense oak tree whose great, spreading arms were covered with pretty ferns. He went up close to the old tree, and to his joyful surprise discovered that the trunk was hollow.

"Would this do?" Moling said to himself. He stepped into the hollow tree. It was high enough to stand up in and just about wide enough to allow him to lie down, and, of course, it would give perfect

shelter from wind and rain when something was done
to block up the opening. The hollow oak was in a
lovely little clearing and near a fine wide river, the
River Barrow.

It was the very hide-out in the very kind of place
that Moling had prayed to find. Immediately he
knelt down on the mossy floor of the forest and
thanked God for having led him to such a wonderful
home, where he had everything he wanted at his
hand : water, fish, herbs, berries, firewood. . . . "Why,
I can live here like a king!" said the simple man.
Kings usually drink nicer things than water and
eat more interesting things than fish and berries—
but never mind.

One of the first things Moling did, after he set
up house in the hollow oak, was to make a little boat
so that he could go fishing on the river. While he
worked at the boat making, he often noticed out of
the corner of his eye that he was being watched by the
animals. Deer and badgers stole up to the edge of
the clearing, curious to find out what all the hammer-
ing was about. The foxes were always coming for a
peep at Moling; they were extremely interested in
all he was doing. When the boat was finished and
brought down to the river, Moling had no more work
to do; nearly all his day was given to praying.

So the wild animals had no fear at all of the quiet man who lived among them and it was not long before they became friendly.

Moling was especially fond of the foxes; he loved their glistening red coats, their bushy tails and their sparkling eyes. He loved to play with the foxes also; he threw them sticks to fetch, he ran races with them and he invented a game rather like hide-and-seek which was the best of fun. Of course the foxes loved Moling, too. When he lay down in his oak house to sleep, the foxes gathered around and slept at the foot of the tree so that they might be near their friend all the time. They would rather die, of course, than do him an injury.

Then everything changed.

One day a man who was searching for stray cattle came upon Moling in the forest. He knew at once that Moling was a holy man living in hiding, and when he got back to the village where he lived he told others of his discovery. They told others and *they* told others; the news spread everywhere. Moling's happy life living in an oak tree and playing with foxes was soon to come to an end. Every day he was disturbed by visitors, people who wanted him to tell them about God, or to bless them, or to pray for their special intentions.

It was bad enough when people came through the forest to find Moling, but others arrived at the opposite side of the river and kept shouting until the worried man answered them. He was such a good man that, instead of telling them to go away, or being rude as you and I might be, he would take out his boat and row across the river to answer all their questions—some of them very silly questions probably. Then worse happened, or worse if you consider the matter from the point of view a fox. Some young men admired Moling so much that they refused to leave him. They built little wooden houses near the oak tree so as to be always close to the holy man. It was only a short time before there was a real monastery in the forest clearing.

The foxes were miserable about the change. The only person they loved and trusted was Moling and now there were many strangers in the place. "Things will never be the same again," said the foxes and most of them ran away into another part of the forest, never to return.

The monks cut down many trees and made the clearing much larger. They dug up the roots, tilled the ground and grew corn and vegetables. The next year they had extra corn so they decided to keep hens. It would be nice, they said, to have a supply of fresh eggs in case a bishop or a king should come to visit us.

One day, shortly after starting on this new venture, a hen was missing. The monk in charge was upset and he went to Moling to report the bad news. Moling immediately remembered his old companions, the foxes. Would they ever be so wicked as to steal hens? Just then he saw a fox lurking at a safe distance among the trees. He called to it and it came slinking forward. Moling looked into the fox's eyes, and he knew.

"Fox," he said, "you are a traitor!"

The fox hung its head with shame.

Moling went on scolding it. "And I thought you were my friend. How often I have fed you with my own hands, how often we have played games together. . . . And now you sneak up here and steal one of our precious hens. I am very disappointed in you. The monks will say that it was very wrong of me to make friends of foxes because they are not trustworthy. . . ."

The fox slunk away and Moling returned to his cell. In a few hours' time the fox returned—with a live hen in its mouth. It placed the hen proudly at Moling's feet.

"Where did you get that one from?" asked the

saint in surprise. Then he examined the hen and all at once guessed what had happened. Some miles away at the edge of the forest, there was a convent of nuns and they, too, kept hens, a special breed with black and white feathers. This was one of the nuns' hens and the fox had stolen it! Once again Moling had to explain to the fox that stealing is wrong and that one

cannot make up for one theft by committing another theft.

"Fox, you and many of your family are my friends, but we won't be friends any more unless you give up stealing." Then Moling told the fox to take the black and white hen back to the nuns and to give up bad habits.

The fox understood and obeyed. The stolen hen was

returned to the convent before anyone even knew it had been stolen! And after Moling's sermon on honesty, no fox ever again touched a hen belonging to monk, nun or anyone else.

Gall's Disobedience

When good people have to live among wicked people, what is the best thing to do? "The remedy is simple," said a saint—not an Irish saint this time but a Spaniard. "You and I must first be what we ought to be; then we shall have cured what concerns ourselves." We are all inclined to talk too much about the wickedness of other people and do nothing to make ourselves perfect.

When Columbanus set out from Ireland to convert the people of France and Switzerland, he knew that the only way to get results was to live a very holy life himself. The pagans in those places were savage, cruel and treacherous; therefore Columbanus and his twelve companions must be meek, kind and reliable. And more than that, they must live like saints, always giving and never taking, praying with their whole hearts and minds.

Columbanus made very strict rules for the twelve monks. They were all, he said, to be satisfied with the simplest food; they were to spend part of the day in prayer, part at reading holy books and part doing the work of the monastery. No matter how tired they were at night, each monk was to pray privately in his cell. And, lastly, if a monk committed even a small sin, he must do penance, maybe fast on bread and water for a few days. When the wild pagans saw how serious the Irish Christians were about their religion, they were impressed and many of them were converted. Soon Columbanus was able to set up schools for the sons of the new converts.

Gall was one of the twelve young monks Saint Columbanus brought with him from Ireland. He was not only a good monk but a clever one; it is said that he was especially clever at grammar, poetry and in knowledge of the Holy Scriptures. And, of course, he was a great missionary. He is honored to this day in Switzerland for the work he did in making the people Christians. But Gall had one little weakness: he was crazy about fishing. Whenever he got a chance, he was off with a rod or a net, casting a line over a rippling river, or trailing a net from a boat on a lake.

Of course it is easy to be a great saint and a keen fisherman at the same time: Saint Peter was. Perhaps Saint Peter was Gall's patron saint—it's funny to think of a saint having a patron saint.

Columbanus and the monks used to find teaching boys at their school rather tiresome at times; boys, you know, get you down. The men longed to be by themselves so that they could pray to their hearts' content. So, every now and again, they left their school at Luxeuil and went off to the "desert." The books call the place the "desert," but I imagine it was just a wild and wooded place, probably on a hillside.

One time Columbanus took Gall with him to this "desert" and there they prayed day and night, living on a few crusts they had brought from the monastery, with, perhaps, the addition of some berries.

"If we had some fish it would be nice," said Columbanus.

The word "fish" was enough to make Gall jump out of his skin with delight. "Fish! Of course! What could be nicer than fish?" Gall sprang to his feet (they had been sitting under a tree eating the dry crusts and the sour berries). "I have my net with me and if you give me leave, I'll soon catch dozens of fish."

"Very well," said Columbanus dryly, for he wasn't

the least keen on fishing. "Take your net and go off and fish in the River Breuchin." He returned to his prayers.

The thought of a day's fishing almost made Gall skip and sing with delight, but suddenly he pulled himself up, remembering his instructions on *where* to fish.

"The River Breuchin—now he *would* say the River Breuchin! It just shows he knows nothing about fishing. The Breuchin is no good. You wouldn't get as much as a pinkeen in it, if you were to net it from end to end." Gall was remembering his boyhood days in Ireland, because "pinkeen" is the Irish name for that tiny, useless fish known elsewhere as the stickleback. "Why didn't he tell me to go and get fish and not mention any special river ... ?"

Then Gall thought of the River L'Ognon. It was a glorious thought and he quite cheered up. *That* river was the really good one and he knew a special pool on it that looked wonderfully fishy. So he hurried on, merely frowning and shaking his head at the River Breuchin as he passed by.

He came to the pool on the River L'Ognon and he cast his net. In less time than it takes to tell, a great shoal of fish swam into the pool. Gall was overjoyed. "I said I would catch dozens, but this looks as if I

am going to catch hundreds, maybe thousands." But he didn't. The fish came to the net and then swung back as if they had faced a wall.

Gall tried the net in another part of the river. Again the shoal swam near the net and again they turned away. Gall was bitterly disappointed. He did not know how to explain the behavior of the fish; it wasn't that they saw the net, because Gall had used the same net many times and had caught plenty of fish in it. They just came up to the net and circled away. He tried another scheme, and another and another. But not a single fish entered the net.

He trailed back to where he and Columbanus were camping. His heart was heavy: no fish and the sin of disobedience. He was told to go to the River Breuchin, not the River L'Ognon. Columbanus saw the young monk coming. He raised his head (for he had been deep in prayer) and though he didn't say a single word, he *looked* a word, "Well?"

"Nothing," answered Gall sorrowfully.

"Nothing?" repeated Columbanus.

"Nothing at all." Gall hung his head and wished that the ground would open and swallow him.

Columbanus asked no more questions. He thought for a while and then he guessed what had happened.

"Why did you not go where you were told? Go back now to the River Breuchin."

And weary as he was, Gall went back. When he reached the bank of the river, he half closed his eyes because he was heartsick. He didn't want to see fish in the water and, in a way, he didn't want to discover that there were *no* fish to be seen. He cast his net without hope and without any of the usual pleasure he had when fishing. The net was hardly in the river before it became heavy; it seemed to weigh a ton. And when he got the net up on the bank, it was bursting with a mass of slithery fish, more fish than Gall had ever netted in his whole life.

There is no need to put an ending to this story. You can imagine how delighted Gall was, you can imagine also how Columbanus smiled when he saw the monk staggering toward him, pulled down to the ground almost with his load of fish from the River Breuchin. I think—though I am not sure—that there was no question of Gall having to do a penance on bread and water. Columbanus forgave him the disobedience. The two of them sat around their camp fire eating lovely fried fish and were as happy as only monks can be.

The Priest and the Bees

Once upon a time there was a good, holy priest, well known to the whole countryside where he lived for his devotion to his priestly work.

He was called out one day to attend a dying man. The priest took the Sacred Host with him to give the sick man Holy Communion, but when he arrived he found that the man was too ill to receive it. He gave the dying man Extreme Unction, prayed by the bedside, gave him his blessing and went away. He did not forget to take the Host with him.

It was the height of summer and a lovely sunny day. The hedges were covered with blobs of snowy white may blossom; the unfolding oak leaves were pure gold; the thrushes were calling out to each other something that sounded like "pretty Joey, pretty Joey," and the blackbirds were whistling as if their hearts would burst with joy. The priest was enjoying his walk. And then he saw something that delighted him altogether: a swarm of bees. The priest was crazy about bees and very clever about managing them; he had nine gleaming straw skeps, or beehives, of bees in his garden near the church.

"And this will make ten—if I can get them!" He was quite excited at the idea.

The first thing to do was to follow the swarm to see where it settled. He must walk fast—he might even have to break into a run—because bees in swarm go this way and that way in a great hurry so that they may find a safe place to spend the night. When the swarm was found in a bush, or hanging to a high branch, he would have to go back to his house to get an empty skep for it. It was indeed a matter of acting quickly, or not acting at all.

The priest laid the Sacred Host on a leaf and placed it on the grass beside the path. He would be sure to remember. . . . Then he ran after the darting, buzzing ball of bees. The swarm dashed over a corn field, then through a grove of birch trees, then across a stream. The priest kept the bees in view all the time, though sometimes he was a long way behind. It was a hot chase and it ended in a peculiar place: his own garden! He was delighted. He quickly got an empty skep and soon, very gently and carefully, had the swarm safe. Bees seemed to be as fond of the priest as he was of them, for he never got stung.

After the happy ending, the priest went into the church to say his prayers and, as he knelt down, he suddenly remembered with a terrible pang that he had forgotten the Sacred Host. He rushed back as fast as he could to the spot where he had first seen the swarm. "On a leaf on the grass by the side of the path. . . ." He looked and looked until darkness came, but he could not find the Host. All night long he prayed and wept, and as soon as it was daylight he went again to the pathway and searched every inch of the ground. There was no sign of the Host.

Days passed like this, praying and searching, going home with empty hands and a heavy heart. The priest became worn and thin. He gave himself hard penances for his forgetfulness; he never ceased to pray. Weeks passed. The poor priest gave up looking for the Host, but he said twice as many prayers and asked twice as much for forgiveness. Months passed. The good priest continued to pray; he was a man of great faith even if he was sometimes forgetful.

A whole year went by. Then one night an angel appeared to him and told him something that filled his heart with hope and joy. The bees saw what had

happened, the angel told him, and when he was removing the swarm from the plum tree in his garden, some of the bees left the swarm and flew back to the Sacred Host. The good little insects got into a bunch and lifted the Host from the leaf and flew off with it to a cleft in a rock nearby.

"Tell me quickly where I am to find the Host," said the priest.

The angel gave him exact instructions and added that it would be a good idea if the priest brought along as many people, Christians and pagans, as possible to see the holy work the bees had done.

Early the next morning the priest rang the bell loud and long, and all the people came running to the church to know what was the matter. "Come with me," he said, "and see a great wonder." They all followed him to the rock near the path. And there, indeed, they saw a great wonder. The bees had not only carried the Host to a safe place, but they built a beautiful shrine for it. They had made a tiny chapel out of wax. In the center and most honorable place, the Host was safe and sound.

The Christian people fell down on their knees and prayed; many of the pagan people were converted, and the priest—but I need hardly tell you how happy he was and how his heart felt as light as a feather. The Sacred Host was brought back in procession to the church and placed in the tabernacle. Then the priest went out to the skeps in the garden and said very gratefully, "Thank you, bees. Thank you very much indeed."

Aengus and the Schoolboy

Aengus was a monk who taught in one of the ninth-century schools. He was said to be first in all Ireland for learning and wisdom. He was a great teacher, but as well as that people were always coming to him for advice on all kinds of things. Far from giving him pleasure, this made Aengus unhappy, because he never had enough time to pray and become holy. Being learned was all right, but being holy was all important.

He made up his mind to be a hermit and live by himself. The abbot did not want to let him go, but at last he gave in. Aengus went off to a lonely place seven miles from the monastery, where he hoped he would not see any more people, or have to answer their difficult questions. But the people began seeking him out at his hermitage in greater numbers than before. At last Aengus felt he could not bear it any longer. He left his hut without telling the monks, or anyone else, what he meant to do. He just disappeared.

He walked for a long time, trying to make up his mind about the best thing to do. Then he happened to pass a graveyard, and as he looked around it, he suddenly stood still with his face shining with joy. He saw a crowd of beautiful angels, more of them than he could possibly count, all clustered over one of the grassy mounds. As he looked and looked, the vision faded.

"That," said Aengus to himself, "must be the grave of a great saint."

He went in to the graveyard to find out the man's name, but there was no stone or anything to show who was buried under the little mound. Aengus then went to the priest's house to find out who had been buried in that grave.

"Only a poor old man," said the priest.

"What special good works did he do?" asked Aengus.

"Nothing that I ever heard of," said the priest. He thought for a moment and then said, "Well, I did hear that when he got up in the morning and again when he was going to bed at night, he used to name all the saints he had ever heard of and ask them to pray for him. That's the only thing special that I ever heard about him."

Aengus said nothing to the priest about the vision he had seen. He went on his way again, thinking about it. It helped him to make up his mind what to do.

"That man," he told himself, "got to Heaven because he was poor and unknown."

Aengus wanted very much to be like that. He knew, however, that he could not be happy anywhere but in a monastery, so he decided to enter one as a servant. Of course it would have to be somewhere where he was not known. In this way he could try to be holy and no one would ever bother him again about his great learning and wisdom.

He went to the monastery of Tallaght, near the city now called Dublin, where he knew he was not known, and there he asked to be taken on as a servant. The abbot agreed and gave Aengus work as a laboring man in the farmyard and mill. No one took any notice of the new servant, who worked hard at the harvest, drawing the sheaves to the barn for threshing, and afterward carrying the sacks of corn to the mill.

Meanwhile, of course, Aengus was missed and his monks sought for him everywhere. News of the disappearance of Aengus spread from school to school and everyone kept a lookout for him, but the monks in Tallaght certainly never imagined he was working among them as a servant. After a time everyone began to think that he must be dead. Seven years passed. Aengus was quite happy. As a poor servant, he was left alone. No one bothered him.

One day a little schoolboy came rushing to him in the barn. He had a miserable face and just stood there looking at Aengus without a word. Aengus guessed, of course, that he had run away from school. He smiled at the boy and began to talk about the weather and the harvest.

"Could I hide here for the day?" said the boy.

"Of course you can," said Aengus, who, as you have seen, really knew a lot himself about hiding.

"Why don't you make a bed there for yourself in the straw? No one could ever find you there unless I told them, and you may be sure I won't."

The boy seemed to think this a great idea. He curled himself up in the straw. "It's the old Latin," he said.

"Oh, do you find it hard?" Aengus asked, thinking of the many, many Latin lessons he had given in the past.

"Hopeless," the boy told him. "It is quite hopeless. I can't go back to school any more. I'm stupid. I can't learn. Then I get punished for something I can't do. I'll have to run away. Maybe you would help me to hide for always?"

His voice trailed away. It was warm and cosy in the straw. He thought this servant had a very kind face. He was tired because he had been dodging all the morning, darting from post to pillar in case one of the teachers would see him. Soon he was fast asleep.

When he woke up some hours later, Aengus was still there, shoveling corn into sacks. He sat down beside the boy and asked him the name of his Latin book. Of course, Aengus knew that whole book off by heart. He began to explain to the boy the lesson which he could not learn. He repeated the Latin sentences from memory and began to turn them into Irish, then back again into Latin. The boy found it interesting. Somehow, it did not seem so hopeless now. He asked questions: *Why* this, that and the other—all the *whys* of that awful Latin! Aengus told him and then it was his turn to question the boy. Soon he found that the boy actually knew the lesson from beginning to end!

The lad jumped up in excitement. "I'm not running away," he said. "I'd like the fellows to hear me at this." He ran to the door.

"Don't tell anyone about this lesson in the barn," Aengus warned him.

"Oh, no, I won't," said the boy.

It was the abbot himself who took this boy's class and next morning it was the abbot's turn to be surprised. Here was the biggest dunce in the class suddenly word-perfect in a difficult lesson! What had come over him? When the class was ended, he called up the boy to him and heard him say the lesson again.

"Who helped you?" he said.

Now the boy had meant to keep his promise to Aengus, but he forgot and blurted out that it was the servant in the barn.

"What made you think of bringing your book out to *him*?" asked the abbot.

"He doesn't have to have the book," said the boy. "He knows it all off by heart." That reply left the abbot speechless. The boy ran off and joined the others at play.

The abbot sat on, thinking hard. What kind of a genuis was that servant who knew the school textbooks by heart? He would be much more useful teaching in the school than carrying sacks on his back. There was only one teacher ever known to have a memory like that.

All at once the truth flashed on him: that servant must be the missing Aengus! A moment later, the boys were astonished to see the abbot running across the playground as if he had wings on his feet. He dashed into the barn calling Aengus by name. He knew by the man's face that he was right and he threw his arms around his neck.

A little later, Aengus agreed to teach again in Tallaght. He and the abbot became great friends. It was a happy day for Ireland when it was known that Aengus was not dead.

Eugene and the Pirates

Suppose that, when you were out walking one day, a tiger jumped out of a bush; or suppose you were attacked by a bull; or suppose robbers broke into your house; or suppose pirates rushed into your school and kidnapped the pupils. . . . Some boys are never done supposing dreadful things of that kind. But pirates *did* rush into Eugene's school and capture the boys, or three of them at any rate.

One day, in the monastic school of Clones, during the morning's lessons when everything was very quiet and, indeed, rather dull, the door of the classroom opened and in walked a band of pirates, armed to the teeth! Eugene happened to be standing up in class reading aloud from the Gospel. There was dead silence for a second and then pandemonium! The boys ran in every direction, knocking things down. Some of them dived out of the room between the pirates' legs. Eugene stuffed the manuscript of the Gospel inside his tunic as he leaped over a bench, but he was not quick enough. He and two of his friends, Tigernach and Coirpre, were captured by the pirates.

There was no one to rescue them. When a monastic school was attacked in this way, the monks' first thought was for the church. No matter who was killed, or captured, the Sacred Hosts in the Tabernacle had to be saved and then, if possible, the altar vessels. This *had* to be done before the pagan raiders could reach the church.

The boys' hands were tied behind their backs and they were marched to the coast where the pirates' boat had been left. The three school friends kept their ears and eyes wide open on that journey overland, seeking for some chance of escape, but they were closely guarded, night and day, and there was no hope of getting away.

They were hustled on board ship and taken overseas to Britain where they were sold as slaves. There were many Christians in Britain who were very sorry for the boys and who said that it was unfair to keep them in slavery. News of their plight reached a great missionary in Scotland, named Ninnian, who was trying to put an end to slavery among his Christian converts. He traveled to the King of Britain and successfully pleaded with him for the boys' release.

As soon as they were free, Eugene and his two friends set off for the coast. They made up their minds that they would wait there until they could get on a boat going to Ireland. They felt sure that they would get help from Christians on the way and their hearts were light. But they had bad luck. When they came within sight of the sea, they saw a boat making preparations to sail. They were helped on board with a kindly welcome and many fair promises. When the boat was far from the shore, however, they found that they were once more prisoners and that they were bound for Brittany, where for the second time they were sold as slaves.

In that country slavery was still the rule, and there was no Christian missionary to come to their help. The master who bought them was not a cruel man, but he believed in getting all the work he possibly could out of his slaves. He set the three Irish boys to grind corn in his mill. They had a steward over them, who was always rushing in and out, shouting to them to hurry, or to pay more attention to what they were doing. It was dusty, disagreeable work, and the boys were kept at it from morning to night every day of the week. When they were allowed to go to bed, they slept until they were shaken again next morning to begin the same round.

In all his adventures, Eugene had managed to hold on to the copy of the Gospel he had stuffed inside his tunic when the pirates rushed into the classroom at Clones. This Gospel now became the boys' most precious possession, their link with the homeland, the sign that they were in reality freemen and Christians. They passed the manuscript from one to the other, guarding it carefully, repeating lines from it to one another, and taking a peep at it whenever they could during their working hours. Even to look at it gave them hope and they prayed with all their might that the Lord would rescue them soon from the hands of their pagan masters. Grown-up people are fond of telling children that their school days are the happiest days of their life. Well, those three boys often said to one another that if only they could get back to their beloved school in Clones, they would never again think the lessons hard, or dull.

One day the steward did not come as usual to the mill. But the boys worked just as hard as ever and by the middle of the afternoon they had a huge heap of corn ground. Eugene then took out his precious manuscript and began reading it to the others, who went on working. But sometimes he came on a word he did not know and then the other two would stop to look over his shoulder and try to help him.

While they were at this, the steward made a surprise visit. He stormed at the boys for their idleness and threatened that if ever he found them behaving like that again, he would punish them severely. By great good fortune, however, he did not take away the book and the boys were thankful for that. As all three of them had by this time made up their minds to be priests when they got their freedom again, they thought that if their only book was taken away from them, they would soon forget how to read. Then their ignorance might prevent them from ever becoming priests.

That night, when they were going to bed, they agreed to pray for the same thing: that God would help them to get even a tiny little rest every day from the endless work of the mill, so that they would get a chance to read and not become altogether ignorant. Next morning, when they began their work, they found to their astonishment that the mill was turning of its own accord. An angel was turning it for them; it was the answer to their prayer! Now they had only to shovel the flour into sacks and take them to the storehouse. They took turns reading the Gospel in between whiles, not forgetting, of course, to keep an anxious watch out for the steward.

This went on for several days. The millwheel was worked miraculously by invisible means; the boys read the Gospel. They began to be almost happy in their captivity. Then one day the steward heard the voice of one of the boys reading aloud. Instead of rushing in, he peeped through a chink in the doorway. The corn was flowing from under the millstone, while all three boys had their heads bent over the manuscript. He could not believe his eyes. Next day he made up his mind that he would watch more carefully. The same thing happened again. The boys did not know that the steward was spying on them. More corn was ground every evening than they could ever have managed themselves, even if they never took their hands from the millstone. The steward told the master, who came to look through the crack in the door. Finally he went in and questioned the boys.

They told him everything, how they wanted to be priests and that they would never succeed if they forgot how to read, and how they had together prayed for time to study. The master began to respect this God of the Christians, Who answered poor slave boys. He gave them their freedom and helped them to get to the coast, where they would find a boat sailing to Ireland. Eugene, Tigernach and Coirpre soon succeeded in getting back again to their own country.

All three of them became monks. And the old ending to the fairy tales will serve here too: they lived happily ever after.

Colman and the Swans

Have you ever heard a swan sing? The only sound I have ever heard them make is a rather frightening hissing, as much as to say they do not like you and would you mind going off about your business.

Numbers of poets have said that swans sing before they die and, if you hear one of them singing, it means the poor thing is about to die and knows it. But the men who really know all about birds only laugh at the poets and say that is nonsense. They say the swan *never* sings, and that one poet just copied from another poet the bit about the swan song because it sounds nice.

However that may be, swans sang for Colman long ago, not once only, but over and over again for many days, and they were not dying swans either.

There were hundreds of saints named Colman in

Ireland of the Golden Age. But the Colman of this story was called Colman of Lann Elo to mark him out from the others of the same name. A great chieftain had given him land for a monastery and school at Lann Elo, now called Lynally, southwest of Tullamore in Offaly. All the buildings in Ireland at that time were made of wood, so the monks' first job was to cut down a large number of trees in order to build huts to sleep in, a schoolhouse and a church. But the place they had selected for the monastery was separated from the forest where the trees stood by a big swamp, or marsh, bordering a lake.

Colman, who was in charge, told them that they would have to make a causeway across the marsh in order to draw the trunks of the trees to the place where they wanted to build.

All the monks had long faces. It is no easy matter to build a road across a swamp. You have to remember that it was hundreds and hundreds of years before the invention of excavators, bulldozers and such mechanical helps. An army of men would be needed to do it fairly quickly because loads and loads of stone would have to be first thrown into the marsh to make a solid foundation for the road. There were only six monks. They knew that it would take months and months of back-breaking work before they would

see their road rising. However, they said nothing,
but cheerfully made a start.

The job turned out to be even worse than they had
feared. For weeks and weeks they did nothing every
day from sunrise to sunset but carry huge stones and
heave them into the swamp. Their hands were soon
blistered, their backs, arms and shoulders ached.
They had to wade into the ice-cold mud with the
stones. It was hard to keep themselves from stopping
to look over to the wood, measuring the distance
with their eyes, trying to count up how much longer
the job would take. They tried, too, not to think of
the other pleasant work they could be doing: tilling
the ground and growing crops, gardening, work the
monks loved because they saw results for it.

Four or five swans on the nearby lake showed
their sympathy with the monks from the first day.
As soon as the work began every morning, they
would swim up from the far end of the water and
cruise slowly around the edge, arching their necks,
watching the toilers. When the monks stopped for
prayer and food, they would throw scraps to the
birds and thus the friendship grew stronger every
day. The only fun the monks had was to watch the
swans in their stately sailing, curling their necks in
the shape of the letter *S,* or up-ending themselves

in comical fashion when they darted their beaks
down to the lake bed for water plants.

One day, after this noon rest, the monks began
work again very slowly. Between their blistered
hands and aching backs, they were in a bad way.
Colman pitied them. The swans were watching in-

tently. It seemed as if they knew Colman's thoughts. One of them began to sing. Colman straightened his aching back and smiled at them encouragingly. The other swans joined in, a sweet, happy song, full of delightful little trills. Smiles passed from face to face. Before they knew it, the monks found themselves working faster. The song had a wonderful effect, making them imagine that they, too, were sailing about in the cool water, happy and rested.

That evening at sundown the toilers reached the edge of the wood with the foundation of their road. Every day after that the swans sang to them to cheer them at the work. When the work was finished, they became the Mute Swans again, birds without song. The place where they sang for so many days is called "Swan's Land" to this day in memory of that event.

Another curious thing happened during the building of the causeway. One spring morning in the middle of the work, Colman fell on his knees in prayer. Then his face became deadly pale and he fainted. The monks ran to him and lifted him up. One of them bathed his forehead with water. At last Colman opened his eyes and said, "Pope Gregory is dead."

Everyone knew how much Colman had loved Gregory, known afterward as *the Great,* who had been a monk and a missionary before he was made Pope. He had done wonderful things for God to deserve his title. He was the leader of all the monks in Christendom and Colman's special hero.

"How do you know that he is dead?" they asked him.

"Because," said Colman, "I heard the bells of Rome tolling for him. He is dead."

The monks looked at one another. "The bells of Rome," they said, "cannot be heard in Ireland."

"Kneel down with me," said Colman, "and I will pray that you, too, may hear those faraway bells."

They knelt on the stones around him and they all heard the sound of church bells tolling. In great grief Colman told them it meant that Pope Gregory had died that morning and was just then being carried to St. Peter's, so they prayed together that his soul might enter Heaven. They wrote down the date, too. It was the 12th of March in the year 604. Later on, they heard from travelers who had come from Rome that Pope Gregory the Great had indeed died and been taken to St. Peter's on that very day.

Loman, the Saint Who Would Not Lend Books

Saint Loman was Saint Patrick's nephew and was among those who traveled with him to Ireland to preach the Christian Faith. When the band of missionaries landed near the mouth of the River Boyne, Patrick set off with some companions to walk to the palace of Tara. He told Loman to mind the boat and steer it up the river as far inland as he could.

It was a weary and rather lonesome task. Loman whiled away the time in chanting psalms and singing all the hymns he knew. Then there came a pleasant break: an Irish boy heard the singing and came to the river bank to see what it was all about. His name was Fortchern. His mother was a Scottish princess and a Christian; his father was a County Meath chieftain and still a pagan. Fortchern and Loman stared at one another for half a minute. Then they

both smiled. As is very often the way with young
boys if they like the look of each other, they made
friends without questions, or fuss. Loman invited
Fortchern into the boat and before you could count

ten, the two of them were singing happily together.

The next thing was that Fortchern's mother up in the fort heard the singing, psalms and hymns that she had known well in her childhood days in Scotland. She could hardly believe her ears! She put everything aside and rushed down to the river. Who was the strange boy seated beside her son in the boat?

"Loman is my name," he told her politely, "and I have come with Patrick to bring the Gospel of Christ to the Irish people."

She was delighted, because she had prayed often and often that God would send missionaries to Ireland. "You must tie up the boat," she said, "and come up to our house for some food."

Later on, Loman became very good friends with this family. After a little while, Fortchern's father also became a Christian. He gave Loman land to build a church near Trim; it was his thanksgiving for the grace of baptism.

Years went by and a great part of Ireland was converted to the Faith. Loman settled down at Trim and became a great scholar and a lover of books. There were not many books in Ireland then about the Christian Faith, so that Loman was the guardian of the written word. It was a position of honor and he took it very seriously. He loved his books so much that he would hardly let anyone take a peep at them, and as for lending one of them—NEVER! Loman said he might not get it back, and indeed he might have been right about that. Loman would give a poor man the clothes off his back, or the last crumb of food in the monastery larder, but books—that was altogether different! They were, he thought, far too precious in a country that possessed so few Christian writings, and he felt it would be wrong to risk losing even one of them.

Now books long ago were not like the books today. If you could go back through the centuries and peep into a monastery library, you would be very surprised at what you saw: no shelves, not a trace of a book to be seen anywhere, just pegs driven into the walls and leather satchels hanging from them. The books, or the manuscripts rather, many of them not bound together at all, were kept in those leather bags so that they would be always dry and clean.

One day Loman got word that Columcille was coming to visit him in Trim. As well as being a very holy monk, Columcille was a prince of the blood royal. He could have been High King of Ireland if he had not chosen to be a priest. But even though he was a priest, he still had a great deal of power and some people were a little afraid of him, because he had an army at his back if he wanted to use it.

Columcille was also well known for his love of books. Indeed, while still a student, he had got into trouble over a book, because he had stayed up all night and copied it without the owner's permission.

Afterward the owner of the book had claimed the copy, too, and there was a dispute. Columcille held on to his copy. The case went before the High King, who took the copy from Columcille, even though he had copied it himself on his own parchment. It was a famous judgment which was repeated all over the schools: *To every cow her calf and to every book its son-book.*

Loman knew all this and he was quite upset when he heard that Columcille was coming to visit him. Although he loved him for many reasons, he did not trust him about books. His first thought was: *My books are not safe. He may even want to borrow them!* So before Columcille arrived, Loman went to his library, gathered all the satchels off the walls and hid them in another part of the monastery.

Columcille arrived and after the usual compliments, when he had taken some food and a rest, he hurried off to the library. What was his surprise to find it empty! He was very disappointed and told Loman he had only meant to *look!* But Loman only smiled. Columcille's visit came to an end and not one single book had he *seen,* let alone touched, or borrowed! But he had a sense of humor and he respected Loman more than ever for being so faithful to his trust.

Loman continued to add to his store of books and to guard them jealously as long as he lived. He wanted the Irish converts to have always in their own country the chief treasures of Christian writing.

On the night of Loman's death, all the book satchels in all the libraries of Ireland fell from their pegs. As the monk librarians picked them up and put them back, they guessed it was a sign that Loman was dead, and they said a prayer for the soul of the greatest booklover in Ireland. If there is ever a patron saint of people who dislike lending books, Loman should be their first choice.

Macanisius and the Child

Colman was a very small boy, able to run about on short, fat legs, but not yet able to speak properly. One day, a terrible thing happened in his home. His father, who was a chieftain, had a bitter quarrel with *his* father. The two men were furiously angry and came to blows. Before anyone could separate them and calm them, the old man was knocked down and the fall killed him. Colman was too young to understand what had happened: his grandfather was dead and it was his father who had killed him!

The ancient Irish took a very serious view of a crime like that, which was understandable, but the punishment for it was a very wrong one. The murderer should see his own son die! This meant that the baby Colman was sentenced to death and that the chieftain would have to see him die. The form of death was a cruel one, too: he was to be tossed into the air, and then ten warriors were to rush forward with their spears lifted up to catch him on the points as he came down.

The Christian bishop of the place, whose name was Macanisius, was very troubled indeed when he heard of this sentence. He knew the family well and liked them. He wanted to save Colman at all costs. As a Christian he knew that the law was unjust, and that an innocent child's life should not be taken to atone for his father's crime. But the early Christians in Ireland found it very hard at first to get the country's laws changed into Christian laws. Even when kings and chieftains became converted to the Christian faith, many of them still held on to the old pagan laws.

Macanisius went around to everyone who had power, begging them to save Colman's life. He went to the judge, pleading to have the sentence changed. He went to the king of that part of Ireland; he went to the High King of all Ireland; he even went to the warriors who were to carry out the sentence. But it was of no use. One and all shook their heads and made the same answer, that the law would have to take its course.

When he failed with men, Macanisius turned to

God. He prayed and prayed that Colman's life might be saved. On the night before the sentence was to be carried out, he stayed up all night praying God to rescue the child. But no one in Heaven seemed to hear him. With a very heavy heart Macanisius went next morning to the field where the little boy was to be killed. A great crowd of idle, curious people had gathered to look on. There was no pity in any face. No one seemed to grieve about the end of a young life except Macanisius.

First the warriors, holding their spears upright, marched into the center of the field. Then the chieftain who had killed his father was led in between two soldiers. He was forced to look on, whether he liked it or not, because that was part of his punishment. Lastly, two warriors brought in Colman, the little boy who was to be the victim. He was too small to understand what was going on and did not in the least suppose that he was going to die. He was laughing as he swung between the warriors' hands.

Macanisius turned away from the place and went up on a little hillock behind the crowd. He felt that his heart would break if Colman was put to death. He prayed more desperately than ever. A strong warrior lifted the little boy in his arms and then flung him high into the air, while ten other warriors lifted their spears to catch him as he came down. Colman should have been spiked to death on those sharp points. But a hurricane arose and whirled him across the field, right over the heads of the people toward the bishop. Macanisius stretched out his arms and snatched the boy.

"He comes from God," he shouted, brave and strong like a warrior. "He is mine now. You cannot take him from me!" Colman hugged him tightly.

There was a great silence for a few seconds and then the crowd roared: "Yes. Let the bishop have him!" They were excited and almost threatening.

The warriors looked at their captain for orders. The captain looked at the judge. The judge turned to the Druids: what did *they* think? But all the while the crowd kept up the roar: "Let the bishop have him!" In the end everyone agreed that what had happened was so strange, it would be wrong to carry out the cruel sentence. The judge told Macanisius he could take the child away. The chieftain, too, was set free.

So the bishop took Colman back with him to the monastery, where the child was brought up as a Christian and where he was always happy. When he grew up, he became a priest and a leader who did great things for the Church of God.

Molua and the Scholars

Saint Molua was abbot, or headmaster, of a school at Kyle, near Borris-in-Ossory. He was famous for his clever way with boys. They all did wonderfully well at his school. He never punished them, never scolded them, never even said a cross word to them. Yet they kept the rules and studied hard. For this reason difficult boys were sent to him from all parts of Ireland.

One day a boy named Conan was brought to him. This lad had been undergoing the very severe training that a poet received in ancient Ireland, when he suddenly decided to change because he wanted to be a priest. He told Molua that he would never, never be able to do any work with his hands. They were delicate, soft hands and the moment he tried to dig, or do anything like that, he got blisters on them. Anyhow, apart from that, Conan hated working with his hands. He knew that he was clever and he said he did not mind how hard he had to study.

"Send him away," advised the other masters. "He's spoiled now. He would never be any use in a monastery if he can't work."

"We'll see," said Molua.

A few days later, he called Conan and told him that they would do some work together in the wood.

"I told you I can't work with my hands," Conan began, almost whining. "Don't ask me to dig, or fell trees, or cut wood. I can't do that kind of thing."

"You'll be able to do this job," Molua promised him. They set off together.

Molua took with him two reaping hooks and a hay fork. Right in the center of the wood was a huge thicket of thistles.

"I want these cleared away," said Molua, "and then we'll have a handy pathway through the wood."

Conan gave a terrified look at the thistles. "I can't," he began. "You see, I have never. . . ."

"Watch me," said Molua, handing one of the reaping hooks to Conan. He pulled forward one single thistle with the fork, holding it conveniently before the lad.

"Cut that," he said. Conan swiped down the thistle with his hook.

"Now that's all we'll do for today," said Molua.

Conan was surprised. "Oh, well," he said, "I could do a bit more than that, you know."

"It's enough for today," repeated Molua.

Next day they cut down just two thistles in the same way. That was all. They returned to the monastery. They cut three thistles the third day, four the next day, five the following day, and on the sixth day they cut six thistles. Each day Conan begged harder to be allowed to do a little more work than was done. He began to feel very much ashamed of himself.

By the end of a fortnight, even though they did so little each day, they had made quite an opening in the grove of thistles. Conan began to be interested in it and to long to get at the job properly. It was three weeks, however, before Molua agreed to let him do so. In a short while the boy cleared the spread of thistles and now the whole school could cross the wood in comfort. Conan ended by removing more than the thistles; he cut back bushes and nettles and made a fine pathway. He was proud when they called it "Conan's Road." Best of all, his hands became strong and hard. He never again complained that he could not work with them.

Another schoolboy, named Colum, went to Molua one day with a ridiculous story about himself. He said that he could not live with a lot of other boys because they kept him from studying, and that the only way he could get the *real good* out of school life was to live by himself, have his own books, his own house and have nothing to do with the others. Molua said gently that it was never good for young boys to be quite alone and that the companionship of the other boys should be a help to him.

"No," Colum insisted, "to get the real good from my study, I must be alone at it."

"All right," said Molua unexpectedly.

So it was arranged. He gave Colum a little wooden house all to himself, with a bed in it and a table to work at. This meant a certain amount of trouble and the other masters grumbled. They said that Colum was just a spoiled brat with a whim and that he would never be cured by giving in to him.

"Wait!" said Molua. "You'll see."

Colum settled happily in the little house where he could be all alone. Things seemed to go well. Then one cold evening, Molua called in to ask how he was getting on. He found the boy sitting before the fire, warming himself.

"Sit down and warm your feet," Colum said pleasantly to the abbot.

"You give me good advice," said Molua, sitting down and holding out his sandaled feet to the cheerful fire. "How are you getting on?"

Colum had no complaint. He was getting the real good out of his study, as he said he would.

Presently Molua got up and stood with his back to the fire. Then he moved about in front of it, as if warming each of his sides. He was keeping all the heat from Colum.

The boy was surprised; Molua was not the sort of man to act in such a selfish way. At last Colum protested, "Why do you stand between me and the fire like that? You are keeping all the heat from me!"

"That's the only way I can get the real good of it," said Molua dryly. "It is no use to me unless I can have it *all* to myself!"

That night the boy thought over Molua's behavior. He knew that the abbot was not selfish. Then he suddenly understood that it was he himself who was selfish, always thinking of himself and no one else. He felt ashamed. Next day he went to Molua and said that he wanted to live again with the other boys and share everything with them. He was cured of his selfishness. He tried to make amends by helping other boys who thought the lessons harder than he did. The masters found him a great help in the school and they were glad then that Molua had taken such trouble with Colum.

Finbarr's Hazelnuts

Saint Finbarr set up a great school for boys in the south of Ireland on a site that later grew into the city of Cork.

One day a most important visitor arrived at the school. His name was Laserian. He was a great missionary and Finbarr's best friend. It was a friendship which had begun when they were both small boys in the same class at school, but they had not met for years and years because Laserian had been far away from Ireland, first in Iona and then in Rome.

Finbarr was overjoyed to see his friend again. He made the day a feast day for the school. The teachers, the boys, the farm workers, the cook, the shoemaker, the miller, absolutely everyone in the place got a free day and a special dinner. There was a smile on every face.

The two friends went for a walk. It was a lovely day in spring. The sun was shining and the first warmth had come to the land. The rooks were busy building their nests, moving over the grass with a hop, skip and a jump, quarreling over twigs and cawing in that excited way they have. The smaller birds were singing in the hedgerows, which were putting out their first tender green. The floor of the woods was golden with pilewort and white with anemones; all the banks were dotted with primroses and violets. The lambs were playing King of the Castle on little knolls in the fields. Spring in Ireland is so lovely that Irishmen find it difficult to imagine how Heaven can be more beautiful.

Finbarr and Laserian were very happy. They had a great deal to talk about. At last they were tired and sat down to rest under a hazel bush. The end of their pleasant time together was drawing near. Laserian was about to leave Ireland again for Rome. It would be a long time before the two friends could have another day together.

Finbarr was well known to be able to work miracles, but he was always trying to hide this power and he did not like people to mention it. Suddenly Laserian said, "Give me a sign that you are favored by God." But Finbarr only shook his head. He told

his friend that to ask for a sign was just silly and that he should have more sense. But Laserian continued to plead. Any little thing would do, he said, by which they would remember that great day. It might be a long, long time before they could meet again.

Finbarr kept shaking his head. He could not deny that he had miraculous power but he did not like to use it except for some very good reason. He tried to be cross with his friend, but he was too happy. And Laserian went on begging for a sign. At last Finbarr looked up at the dusty yellow hazel catkins over their heads. He raised his hand in blessing and at once all the catkins fell off, powdering their heads with the yellow pollen. Instead, there were nuts on the branches, ripe nuts in March, six months before they were due! While Laserian was brushing the catkins from his hair, Finbarr stretched up his hand and picked a cluster of nuts. He threw them at Laserian.

"There's your sign," he said, laughing.

They heard the far-off tinkle of the monastery bell. It was time to go back. They scrambled to their feet. Laserian held the branch of hazelnuts as if it were a holy thing.

"I am sorry if I teased you," he said to his friend.

"I know well that you are favored by God without any sign to tell me."

But he carried the hazelnuts away with him and he kept them always. Whenever he looked at them, he saw Finbarr's face in the spring sunshine. Wherever he was, he had only to look at that little bough and he felt he was back in Ireland again. It was a keepsake that Laserian loved to the end of his life.

Date Due